What Was Cooking in Mary Todd Lincoln's White House?

Tanya Larkin

The Rosen Publishing Group's
PowerKids Press™
New York

The recipes in this cookbook are intended for a child to make together with an adult.

Many thanks to Ruth Rosen and her test kitchen.

Published in 2001 by The Rosen Publishing Group, Inc.
29 East 21st Street, New York, NY 10010

First Edition

Book Design: Danielle Primiceri
Layout Design: Emily Muschinske

Photo Credits: pp. 4, 11, 13, 15, 21 © Bettmann/CORBIS, pp. 7, 9, 17. 19 © Dean Galiano.

Larkin, Tanya.
    What was cooking in Mary Todd Lincoln's White House? / Tanya Larkin.
        p. cm.— (Cooking throughout American history)
    Includes index.
    Summary: This book describes Mary Todd Lincoln, wife of the sixteenth president of the United States, her role as first lady, and some of the foods she served at various stages of her life. Includes recipes.
    ISBN 0-8239-5609-1
    1. Cookery, American—Juvenile literature. 2. Lincoln, Mary Todd, 1818–1882—Juvenile literature. [1. Lincoln, Mary Todd, 1818–1882. 2. First ladies. 3. Women—Biography. 4. Cookery, American.] I. Title. II. Series.
    2000
    641.3'00973—dc21

Manufactured in the United States of America

Contents

A Strong and Lonely Woman

Mary Ann Todd Lincoln may have been one of the loneliest and most unhappy first ladies to live in the White House. Mary and her husband, Abraham Lincoln, lived through difficult times. Abe Lincoln became the 16th president of the United States in 1860, just before the beginning of the **Civil War**. The war lasted all through Abe Lincoln's first **term** in the White House and during the first months of his second term. Throughout the war years, Mary Lincoln carried out her duties as the White House **hostess**. She enjoyed welcoming guests to the White House, although many people **criticized** her for doing so. It was wartime. People thought that money used for entertainment should go toward the war effort.

◀ *This portrait shows Abraham Lincoln, 16th president of the United States, and his wife Mary Todd Lincoln.*

5

The Couple From Kentucky

Mary Todd and Abraham Lincoln were both born in the **frontier** state of Kentucky. Mary was the daughter of a rich, important family in Lexington, the state capital. She was well-educated and she had strong opinions. As a young woman, she bragged that, someday, she would marry a man who would become president of the United States. Abraham Lincoln came from a different kind of background. His father was **illiterate**. Growing up, Lincoln lived in a one-room log cabin in Kentucky's woodsy frontier. Young Abe loved to read. During a visit to Springfield, Illinois, Mary was introduced to Abe. He had become a lawyer by then. Mary was attracted to the very tall man who was 11 years older than she.

Spicy Sour Cream Cookies

You will need:

2 eggs
1 cup (237 ml) sugar
¾ cup (177.4 ml) sour cream
2 cups (473 ml) sifted flour
½ teaspoon (2.5 ml) baking soda
¼ teaspoon (1.2 ml) cinnamon
¼ teaspoon (1.2 ml) nutmeg
2 tablespoons (30 ml) butter
2 cups (473 ml) sifted confectioners' sugar
¼ cup (59 ml) evaporated milk

HOW TO DO IT:

☞ Have an adult heat the oven to 375 degrees Fahrenheit (191° C)

☞ Sift together flour, baking powder, and salt in a mixing bowl.

☞ Beat the eggs.

☞ Add the sugar and sour cream. Mix well.

☞ Combine the flour, baking soda, cinnamon, and nutmeg.

☞ Add to the egg mixture. Stir until blended.

☞ Drop a teaspoon (ml) of dough onto a greased cookie sheet.

☞ Bake 8 to 10 minutes. Makes about 50 cookies.

Brown Butter Icing:

☞ In a saucepan, melt the butter until it turns light brown.

☞ Stir in the sifted confectioners' sugar

☞ Add the evaporated milk.

☞ Stir until well blended. Pour over hot cookies.

These were popular cookies on the Kentucky frontier.

The Springfield Years

Mary and Abe married in 1842. Her family didn't think he was good enough for her. Their son Robert was born a year later. Their second son, Edward, died at the age of three. William, who was always called "Willie," was born in 1850. Thomas was born three years later. He was called "Tad," because when Tad was born, his large head and thin legs made him look like a tadpole. Abe had served in Congress since 1835. For many years, Mary and their sons remained in Illinois, while Abe worked in Washington. Even without her husband, Mary loved to entertain. She often invited as many as 70 people to her home after church for her strawberries-and-cream parties.

Chocolate-Dipped Strawberries

1 pint (0.5 liters) of large, fresh strawberries

¼ cup (30 ml) shortening

1 oz (198 gm) bar of bittersweet or milk chocolate

HOW TO DO IT:

- ☞ Carefully rinse off strawberries, dry, and set aside.
- ☞ Slowly melt the chocolate and shortening in a small saucepan over a low fire.
- ☞ Remove chocolate from heat as soon as it melts. Do not overcook.
- ☞ Pour chocolate into a heat-resistant dish.
- ☞ Dip each strawberry into the chocolate until it is covered halfway.
- ☞ Place chocolate-dipped strawberries onto a piece of waxed paper.
- ☞ Place them in the refrigerator to set. Or eat right away.

Mary Lincoln liked to serve strawberries in many ways. She might have loved these easy-to-make chocolate-dipped strawberries.

President and First Lady Lincoln

When Abraham Lincoln was elected president in 1860, Mary was excited about becoming the new first lady. People elected Abraham Lincoln because he was "**folksy**." He was known as an honest **politician**. He had also become known for his ideas against **slavery**. Mary Lincoln supported her husband's concerns about slavery. People living in the country's southern states believed that slavery was necessary for their way of life. Slavery was against the law in the northern states. As new states joined the **Union**, Lincoln was against any new state being admitted as a "slave state."

Abraham Lincoln was a popular politician. When he ran for president, he discussed his concerns about slavery. ▶

Mary Goes Shopping

When the Lincolns arrived in Washington, they found the White House in poor condition. The furniture was dirty. The carpets were worn thin. Mary immediately asked Congress for $20,000 to **renovate** her new home. Despite grumblings by many people in and out of the government, Congress gave her the money. Mary went on a shopping **spree** in New York. She bought expensive vases, furniture, and other decorations. She also bought expensive gowns for herself. She wanted to impress the important people in Washington. She was criticized for her spending. Some people said that Mary Lincoln was "just a dowdy **pioneer**" woman. They made fun of her gowns, which were cut low at the neck. They even made fun of the fresh flowers she wore in her hair for formal events.

Mary Lincoln liked to dress in beautiful gowns for her parties. Some people made fun of her low-cut gowns and the fresh flowers she often wore in her hair. ▶

A Troubled White House

Mary Lincoln soon had much more to worry about than what people thought of her expensive gowns. Months after the Lincolns moved to Washington, seven southern states **seceded** from the United States. They elected their own president and formed a new country. The new country was called the **Confederate** States of America. Mary's brothers and other male relatives in Kentucky were in the Confederate Army. Some northerners thought Mary was a traitor or a spy. At the same time, plantation owners in Virginia and Maryland, and some people in Washington, D.C., who sided with the South, avoided the Lincolns.

Abraham Lincoln often visited Union soldiers on the battlefield. ▶

Mary's Important Guests

The Lincolns had many opportunities to enjoy the company of famous and interesting guests. Mary invited several Native American Indian chiefs to the White House. She also entertained Ralph Waldo Emerson who was a famous **essayist**. Another guest was Julia Ward Howe, who wrote "The Battle Hymn of the Republic," **anthem**. During the Civil War, this anthem was sung by people who supported the Union. Mary Lincoln invited Frederick Douglass to have tea with the president. Douglass was a former slave who had written books and was an **abolitionist**. Mary was the first wife of a president to entertain a black person in the White House.

Coconut Macaroons

You will need:

5⅓ cups (1.26 liters)
　　flaked coconut
14 oz (414 ml) can
　　sweetened condensed
　　milk
2 teaspoons (10 ml)
　　vanilla extract
1½ teaspoon (7.4 ml)
　　almond extract

HOW TO DO IT:

☞ Have an adult heat the oven to 350 degrees
　　Fahrenheit (177° C).
☞ Combine all ingredients in a large bowl.
☞ Mix well.
☞ Drop dough with a teaspoon onto a foil-lined,
　　greased cookie sheet.
☞ Bake 8 to 10 minutes, until edges are light brown.
☞ Remove from cookie sheet immediately.
☞ Cool on a wire rack.
　　Makes 3 dozen cookies.

When guests came to tea at the White House, Mary
Lincoln liked to serve them macaroons.

17

A White House Ball

In February 1862, the Lincolns hosted their first large ball. Everyone wanted to attend this event. The guest list grew from 500 to 1,000. The tables were piled with different kinds of game, like quail, duck, and turkey. Game is wild animals that are hunted and caught for eating. Abe Lincoln ate little meat, but he enjoyed a special chicken with gravy recipe. The desserts included models of a 40-gun battleship made of sugar, and a sugar beehive filled with pudding. While Mary prepared for this event, her sons Willie and Tad lay ill in their rooms with **typhoid fever**. Mary and Abraham Lincoln greeted their many guests with smiles, but they were concerned about their children upstairs.

Chicken for Company

You will need:

1 lb (454 gm) skinless
   chicken cutlets
½ cup (118 ml) flour
½ cup (118 ml) vegetable
   oil
½ pint (118 ml) heavy
   cream
¼ teaspoon (1.23 ml)
   nutmeg
parsley
salt and pepper to taste

HOW TO DO IT:

☞ Wipe off chicken cutlets with a damp paper towel.

☞ Season the cutlets with salt and pepper.

☞ Place flour on a flat plate. Dip chicken cutlets into the flour until each is completely covered.

☞ Heat vegetable oil in a frying pan over medium heat.

☞ Carefully place chicken cutlets into the pan.

☞ Cook until browned on each side.

☞ Turn off heat and place cutlets onto a clean plate.

To Make Gravy:

☞ Pour off some of the drippings in the frying pan.

☞ Add the cream, nutmeg, salt, and pepper.

☞ Roll a teaspoon (5 ml) of butter into flour.

☞ Mix and bring to a boil over medium heat.

☞ Pour over chicken pieces.
   Serve with parsley.

Mary's Grief

Young Tad recovered from his illness. Although Mary and Abe took turns sitting by Willie's bed, their 11-year-old son died two weeks after getting sick. The president tried to comfort his wife, but Mary was heartbroken. She would no longer allow the Marine Band to play concerts on the White House lawn because Willie had enjoyed music. She also kept fresh flowers out of the White House because her son had loved them. Mary never recovered from Willie's death. She tried to fill his absence by spending money on shopping sprees. When Mary ran up a **debt** of $27,000, newspapers wrote unkind articles about her. The president had to pay her bills out of his own pocket.

Tad Lincoln, posing here with his father, Abraham, was called "my troublesome sunshine," by his mother, Mary. ▶

Lincoln Is Killed

On April 14, 1865, President Lincoln woke up happy. The Civil War had ended a few weeks earlier. The Lincolns' oldest son, Robert, was home from the battlefield. Abe and Mary had breakfast with their sons. That evening Mary and Abe attended a play at Ford's Theatre. During a moment of laughter in the audience, Abraham Lincoln was shot by John Wilkes Booth. Booth hated the North. He was angry that Lincoln had ended slavery. A badly wounded Lincoln was carried to a house across from the theater. He died the next day. Lincoln's body was carried by train to Springfield, Illinois, for burial. Once again Mary was sick with grief. After her husband's death she wrote, "There never was a more loving and devoted husband." Mary Lincoln later returned to Springfield where she lived another 17 years. She died in 1882 in the house where she had been married.

Glossary

abolitionist (ah-buh-LIH-shun-ist) A person who worked to end slavery.

anthem (AN-thum) A sacred song or hymn.

Civil War (SIH-vul WOR) The war between the northern and southern states of America, fought from 1861 to 1865.

Confederate (kun-FEH-deh-ret) People who fought for the South during the Civil War.

criticized (KRIH-tih-syzd) To find fault with.

debt (DEHT) To owe other people money.

essayist (EH-say-ist) A person who writes short articles about a specific subject.

folksy (FOK-see) To behave in a friendly, casual manner.

frontier (frun-TEER) The edge of settled country, where the wilderness begins.

hostess (HOS-tes) A woman who gives parties and invites guests.

illiterate (ih-LIT-uh-ret) Unable to read or write.

pioneer (PY-uh-neer) One of the first people to settle in a new area.

politician (pah-lih-TIH-shun) A person who holds or runs for office.

renovate (REH-noh-vayt) To repair and restore to make better.

seceded (sih-SEED-ed) To withdraw from an organization or a country.

slavery (SLAY-ver-ee) The system of one person "owning" another.

spree (SPREE) A period of activity or fun, especially when it is overdone.

term (TURM) The limit of time one can be in office.

typhoid fever (TY-foyd FEE-ver) An infectious and often deadly disease that is usually caused by unclean food and water.

Union (YOON-yun) The northern states during the Civil War.

Index

Web Sites

To learn more about Abraham and Mary Todd Lincoln, check out these Web sites:

http://www.firstladies.org/MARY_LINCOLN/FL.HTML

http://www.nps.gov/liho/home/home/htm